11226

When Your Friend Needs You

PAUL WELTER

POCKET GUIDES
Tyndale House Publishers, Inc.
Wheaton, Illinois

When Your Friend Needs You is adapted from *How to Help a Friend* by Paul Welter © 1978 by Paul Welter, published by Tyndale House Publishers, Inc.

First printing, October 1986
Library of Congress Catalog Card Number 86-50745
ISBN 0-8423-7998-3
© 1986 by Paul Welter
Printed in the United States of America

CONTENTS

Introduction: Caring or Meddling? . . . 5

ONE
Three Kinds of Needs 11

TWO
How Predicaments Start 33

THREE
Helping an Inexpressive Friend 42

FOUR
Helping an Impulsive Friend 57

FIVE
Helping an Indecisive Friend 70

Appendix: Learning Channels 83

Caring or Meddling?

Imagine yourself in the following situations:

1. There is an elderly woman living next door whose husband died a month ago. At first she had many friends and relatives who came by. Now the callers have dwindled and you have not seen anyone come by for the last several days. You know she is lonely and needs to talk. You think about going over to see her, but you wonder what to say.

2. You go to the lounge in your office for coffee and a man comes in and sits near you. You have heard that his thirteen-year-old boy was diagnosed last week as having leukemia. The two of you begin to talk first about the weather and then about how things are going in the office. You both sense a need to talk about the topic that is foremost in your minds. You wait for him to bring it up and then you realize that he may be avoiding talking about his son because he thinks it might make you uncomfortable.

3. A good friend is getting a divorce. She told you last week that it would be finalized

today. You know that she will be especially lonely and needing to talk. What should you say?

4. You and your husband are good friends of a couple who are having some stormy times. Last time you dropped by, the man was gone and his wife explained that he was out drinking. Thinking she needed to explain further, she said, "Oh, he's not an alcoholic, he just has a drinking problem." But she goes on to say that now she's scared when he comes home drunk. She is fearful of the future. She looks at the two of you and asks, "What can I do?"

You have probably had one or more experiences of this type. As you read through the above situations and saw yourself as the helper or the potential helper, how comfortable did you feel in that role? How confident did you feel about your skills? Would you have taken the initiative in helping? Would you see your intervention in these situations as meddling or caring?

WHY PROFESSIONALS AREN'T ENOUGH

There are relatively few professional counselors to meet the needs that exist among hurting people today. Unlike a general practitioner, the professional mental health worker is able to see perhaps only six persons per day for an hour each.

Besides the problem of a relatively small number of professional mental health workers, who each can carry only a small case load, we have the problem of many persons who will not consent to see a professional counselor even when they need help. They do not want to reveal parts of their private life, in much the same way that many people resist going to a physician for a complete physical because they would have to take off their clothes. Still others refuse to go because they believe that seeking a professional counselor is an announcement to relatives or friends that they are mentally ill.

Ministers meet the counseling needs of many persons. But nearly all ministers have a preaching ministry and administrative work in addition to their pastoral ministry, so they are limited in the amount of time they can spend in counseling. Moreover, some pastors lack confidence in their counseling skills, and this lack of confidence reduces the amount of time they choose to spend in counseling.

For whatever reasons, many persons who need help desperately will not receive it from a professional counselor or minister.

FILLING THE GAP: FRIEND-HELPERS

Phil is a twenty-three-year old man who is married and has a job. He is involved in a predicament right now because he is having difficulty adjusting to the responsibilities of marriage, and he doesn't like his job.

The chances are that he may not have a person with helping inclinations and skills among his daily associates. Because people are more mobile now, he is less likely to have parents and grandparents readily available than used to be the case. And because a minority of persons attend church regularly, he may not have an ongoing relationship with a pastor. Phil, therefore, is left without help from persons in the mainstream of his daily life. And until his predicament reaches crisis proportions, he is unlikely to seek help from persons he doesn't even know.

We need people who are prepared to help their friends. We need to have competent persons "at the scene of the accident." To carry the medical analogy further, non-professional helpers can provide psychological first aid, but they can do far more than this—they can make a *long-term* positive difference in the lives of their friends.

A person who reaches out to help someone who is psychologically close already has met the first prerequisite of successful caring—a friendly relationship. Whether it is referred to as involvement, a "therapeutic" relationship, or respect, it is something that good friends have been doing for a long time.

Some people believe that a friendly relationship actually precludes one person from providing help to another. The early psychoanalysts who sat behind the reclining patient and maintained a social and psychological distance were examples of this point of view. They thought the helper had to be inscrutable, distant, mysterious, and functioning more in a role than as a person.

Fortunately, the contemporary helper is much more likely to want to get involved and to let the other person see him or her not just as a minister or psychologist, for example, but as a *person*. In fact, it is becoming clear that in the real crises of life, we help best when we mentally shed our helping labels and roles and simply allow one life to touch the other. This does not mean we put aside our skills, which are very necessary for helping. Rather it means that we have integrated these skills into our way of living, so they have become a part of us rather than just a way of behaving we adopt to help someone.

SKILLS TAKE PRACTICE

Counselors in training often report that their wives or husbands or children say to them, "Don't counsel me," or "Now you're talking like a counselor." There are usually two reasons for these reactions.

First, the person who is learning counseling skills may be changing significantly the way he talks. Perhaps he needs to. And because he talks in a different way, he sometimes comes across as unnatural.

A second reason is that beginning counselors feel artificial about the skills they are learning. This does not mean the skills are not real and helpful. For example, when we are learning a new physical skill, whether it's a tennis serve or a golf swing, it feels artificial at first; later it becomes automatic.

As you learn, through practice, the skills that are taught in this guide, you may feel clumsy and artificial at first. But don't give up. If you keep working at incorporating them into your life, they will become natural and automatic.

There is no substitute for patience and determination in your quest to acquire helping skills. But the outcome is worth it. Gaining greater insights and skills in this area can serve to positively change your own life. And it will enable you to become a far more effective helper when your friend needs you.

Three Steps to Helping a Friend
1. Assess the urgency of the other person's need. Is he or she involved in a problem, predicament, or crisis? (See chapter 1.)
2. If the urgency is great, respond in a way that will meet the immediate need. If the situation is not so urgent, work to understand that person better. What strengths and weaknesses led to his predicament? (See chapters 2-5.)
3. Understand how your friend learns. What method of communication will best help him or her? (See appendix.)

Three Kinds of Need

To become an effective helper, you should be able to *recognize* the level of need of a friend who wants your help. These levels are described in the accompanying chart, "Levels of Need."

Problem. The term "problem" is often used as a catchall to describe every kind of difficult human situation. However, we will use it in a *precise way* to refer to the easiest level of need. As the dictionary points out, a problem has a solution. Let's suppose you have a friend, Pat, who moved to town recently. She calls you saying she doesn't feel well, and she asks for suggestions for a family physician. As the chart points out, often information is all that is needed in a problem situation. You suggest several names to her, and she sets up an appointment with one of these physicians. You have solved her problem.

Predicament. Pat comes over for coffee one morning during the following week. She tells you the doctor could find no physical cause for her discomfort. He believes she

LEVELS OF NEED

LEVEL AND DEFINITION	CHARACTERISTICS OF THE PERSON IN NEED	EFFECTIVE HELPING RESPONSES
Problem: Has a solution.	Asks specific question; wants immediate advice or information.	Supply information or advice.
Predicament: Has no easy or satisfactory solution.	Often feels trapped; is not helped by information or advice.	Get involved; use "tender-tough" caring approach.
Crisis: Is a very large predicament; usually short-termed.	Has a sense of urgency; may both want and not want help.	Exercise perceptiveness to sense the state of crisis; intervene; get in touch.

is suffering from anxiety, and he has recommended she take tranquilizers for awhile. She is opposed to taking tranquilizers, yet she feels miserable in her present condition. She is now immersed in a situation for which there are no easy or satisfactory solutions.

Giving suggestions and advice, which worked in her previous *problem*, does not help her now because she feels trapped. She is now at the *predicament* level. You will need to shut off advice-giving and seek a deeper involvement with her. Let her know you care by your attentive listening. By just being a friend to her and providing a listening ear, you may help her reduce her level of anxiety.

Crisis. Let's suppose, however, that her predicament deepens. Later you are at a lunch counter in a downtown department store with her. She cries as she tells you that things have gotten worse during the last week. Her family is tired of her edginess, and she is sick of their yelling—and she is afraid. She doesn't know what will happen to her.

Pat is now in a state of *crisis*. You will notice on the chart that this is a difficult, usually short-term situation, a very large predicament with a sense of urgency. The most helpful thing you have to give in a crisis is your presence. The caring presence of a friend may help a person slow down, avoid rash decisions, and seek professional help, when necessary.

Let's discover some ways to help a friend at each of the above need levels.

WHEN YOUR FRIEND HAS A PROBLEM

We just referred to Pat, who wasn't feeling well and called for suggestions in selecting a family physician. She was fairly new to town and didn't want to limit herself to the information in the yellow pages for making such an important decision.

Pat had a *problem*. We are using the term in the same limited way the dictionary uses it—a situation that has a solution. Most problems that require counsel are not problems at all, but predicaments or crises. It is absolutely crucial for the helper to distinguish between a problem and a predicament or crisis. Otherwise he will "help" in a way that is neither desired nor helpful.

RECOGNIZING PROBLEMS

A person asks you for advice. One clue that the situation may be a problem comes when someone asks your advice. A problem is the only one of the three levels of need that can be remedied by advice. Advice will usually help move the person toward a solution in a problem situation.

It is not always true that one who asks for advice has a problem. If a friend asks you what he should do in a certain situation when he knows what he needs to do but wants you to take the responsibility for the decision, he is really involved in a predicament rather than a problem. This predicament has stemmed from a deficiency in his life—a weak choosing channel. Advice given in this situation would tend to weaken your friend further because it carries the message, "You really *aren't* able to make your own decision."

Your advice meets no resistance. Suppose your friend says to you, "I have this problem. I'm overweight. Nothing seems to work in helping me lose weight. What would you suggest?" In reply you give three or four ideas you think might be helpful.

If your friend accepts these as worthwhile suggestions to think about, then he probably really wants advice. On the other hand, if he meets each suggestion with a "Yes, but—" then the chances are he may not really be seeking advice. If you find yourself urging someone to do something or to take some suggestion, this indicates that there is defensiveness or resistance in the other person: it shows he has a predicament rather than a problem.

Involvement is not required. Anyone with accurate information can help a person who has a problem. One chain of service stations has used the motto, "As you travel, ask us." People who are lost can stop in and ask directions. In this case, they receive help in their problem from a person they don't even know. However, most of us prefer to get information from a friend, if possible.

Someone may have difficulty starting a car and you stop and give a suggestion that helps him get the engine started. You have solved his problem for him. One person can solve a problem for another person. This is the only one of the three levels at which one person can take care of the situation for another person.

THE FIRST HELPING STEPS

Although a problem situation is the easiest need level to work with, it's still possible to blow your opportunity to help. By using the approach shown here, you can increase the chances that your interaction will be genuinely helpful.

1. *Be sure you understand the problem* and the specific nature of the help being asked for. This requires very careful listening on your part and probably some dialogue between the two of you until you are *sure* what the person wants.

2. *Respond to the problem.* If you have the information, provide it. If you don't have it and are willing to do the necessary research or work to get it, let the person know when you will get back to him. If what you are giving is an opinion rather than a fact, label it that way.

Let's suppose at work you have noticed that another person who is fairly new on the job typically does things the hard way. One day he says to you, "I'm always beat at the end of the day, but you seem to get through the day in pretty good shape. How do you manage that?" At this point you can share your observations and suggest more efficient procedures to help him with his problem of fatigue. If you can give this information in a brief, easy, matter-of-fact way rather than lecturing him, he will be more likely to use it.

FOLLOW-UP

If you are giving advice or information to a person whom you know and whom you will be encountering again, it is a sign that you care if you ask later how the situation worked out. This follow-up will also help you because you will begin to put together a set of experiences that show when advice is helpful and when it is not.

Follow-up is a key concept in helping. It is a logical outgrowth of a point of view that we *can* make a difference in a friend's life as our lives flow together over a period of time. It is much different than looking around for persons to help in a single encounter with no thought of seeing them again.

WHEN YOUR FRIEND HAS
A PREDICAMENT

Imagine that you are locked in a dark room and that you have been calling for help. You have been unable to get out, and no one has responded to your calls. You sit down, discouraged, then get up and call out again. Finally you hear an answer to one of your calls. The person who has heard you checks the door but finds it is locked from the *inside*.

The presence of another human being encourages you, and the information that the door is locked from the inside provides some insight. You get down on your hands and knees and feel on the floor with your fingers for a key. Finally, you find it; you rush to the door, unlock it and regain your freedom.

Who got you out, you or your friend? Well, you unlocked the door. On the other hand, you were unable to get out before your friend came along.

This situation illustrates a saying that is used by Integrity Therapists: "You alone can do it, but you can't do it alone."[1] This is a saying that generally holds true for predicament situations. The person involved in the predicament is the only one who can get himself out. However, he needs a helper who will be with him, get involved with him, and talk with him.

RECOGNIZING PREDICAMENTS

No solution is apparent. A predicament is a situation with no easy or satisfactory solution. In an earlier section a situation was used in which Pat, a neighbor, tells you she has seen her physician who could find no physical cause for her discomfort. He has recommended she take tranquilizers. She is opposed to this; however, she feels very anxious and "edgy." So she doesn't know what to do; there is no good alternative apparent to her.

The person feels trapped. Because she can see no way out, Pat becomes aware of something that is happening to her emotionally—

she is beginning to feel trapped. The trapped feeling brings with it some twinges of hopelessness. The situation may look to you more like a problem than a predicament. But the level of need is a function of *how the situation looks to the person in the middle of it*. Therefore, to determine the level of a person's need, you will have to look at the situation through the other person's eyes.

The urgency is not great. People generally feel quite uncomfortable in a predicament. It may last a long time or only a short time. It differs from a crisis in that a crisis, although usually of shorter duration, is much more threatening and therefore produces a sense of dire urgency. In a crisis the involved person knows that something *has* to be done right away. The person in a predicament knows that something *needs* to be done, but he usually does not feel the pressure of time so keenly.

THE FIRST HELPING STEPS

I'M WITH YOU

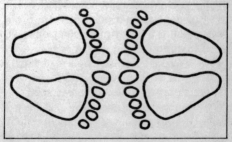

1. *Get involved.* An important way to work with persons in a predicament is to get involved with them. This means we talk with them, listen to them, and do some activities together. So with Pat, for example, the helper would need to get involved with her when she finds that there is no physical cause for her misery. She may be plagued by anxiety or loneliness and she needs a friend who is willing to invest time in her.

```
TAKE
MY ADVICE:
I WON'T
BE
USING IT!
```

2. *Avoid giving advice.* A student in the middle of a predicament came into my office and opened the conversation by saying, "I came to see you because I knew you wouldn't give me pat answers." Most people in predicaments do not want advice, perhaps because nearly all advice is from the giver's, not the *user's*, point of view. Advice works with a problem because it has a solution that does not depend on a point of view. But a predicament is a vastly more complex situation than a problem.

Have you had the experience of urging someone to do something and feeling his resistance? If we come up behind someone and push him, the chances are that he will dig his heels in right away. Most people don't want to be pushed. Newton's Third Law of

Motion applies here: "For every action there is an equal and opposite reaction." When we advise somebody to do something, or push someone toward some action, that person will usually push back and resist. The helper therefore must find some other way to help than by giving advice.

3. *Work for openness rather than closure.* One reason we often give advice is that we want the other person to get the matter settled, to get on with it, to make the decision. Psychologically, we push for closure in many things. If we see a partially formed geometric design, we tend to close it in our minds. This tendency works well for us sometimes, and rather badly at others. Giving help is one venture in which working for speedy closure is usually nonproductive and sometimes even counterproductive.

Suppose your friend is involved in a predicament concerning her elderly father who has been living alone but is rapidly losing the ability to care for himself. There are two or three options open as a place for him to live.

It is tempting to help your friend get all

the information regarding each option and arrive at a rational decision regarding each option as rapidly as possible. After all, the decision cannot be put off indefinitely. We often tend to see a person like this as being in a predicament regarding a *decision*.

However, the predicament may be much deeper than the rational decision-making process. It may involve a psychological journey for your friend in which she moves from a "child" position in relation to her father to a position of care-giver or guardian of her father. To bypass this tremendous psychological need in a push for closure would do your friend a disservice.

If we go into the helping venture without a personal need to arrive quickly at a solution, we will listen much more carefully and will be far more open to where our friend is psychologically. Usually as we adopt this position, we help our friend to make the personal growth and necessary changes in points of view so she can begin to make decisions.

RESPECT: THE BIG R

4. *Show respect.* It is unlikely that we will be able to help a person whom we do not

respect. If we feel our friend is "making a mountain out of a molehill," then this impatient attitude of ours comes across as a lack of respect. If we can't understand why it takes a person so long to make a decision, our arrogance may be taken as a lack of respect.

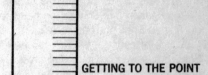

GETTING TO THE POINT

5. *Be concrete.* One of the characteristics of an effective helper is that he gets to the point; he is specific. The helper is able to share his own actual feelings. He avoids abstractness and favors concrete, substantive communication. Instead of saying, "I can see where this situation with your family has you in a dilemma," he may respond, "It looks as if you don't know what to do next because you and your husband don't agree on how to discipline your youngest child." As the helper becomes concrete, he enables his friend to talk more concretely and think more concretely. Thinking in concrete terms makes the predicament much more manageable.

The barrier to concreteness is usually not a lack of language skills; it is rather that we are purposely vague. We pull our punches because we think we may hurt the other person, or because we lack courage to risk possible misunderstanding.

Actually most people are quite resilient and we can say the truth in the plainest way possible without harming them. The exception to this occurs when we *want* to hurt the other person. If this is the case, the chances are we will hurt them no matter how much we disguise the truth. If we feel any need at all to get revenge or to "teach them a lesson," of course we need to back off fast and not pretend to help.

A lack of courage was mentioned above. Sometimes we convince ourselves that the other person is fragile and cannot stand the truth, when the fragility is within *us*. It is not that the other person can't bear the truth, but that he *won't* bear it. The human personality is strong—able to bear the truth when it is clearly stated in a loving way.

FOLLOW-UP

The follow-up in a predicament can be done in a more relaxed way than in a crisis. But it is necessary to follow up and see how your friend is feeling and functioning.

The example was given above of a friend who was faced with her father's declining health and the need for a different place to live. Making yourself available to your friend at a later time to talk about this predicament again will be important. Along with this, we need to remember that there will be times when our friend does not choose to talk about her predicament, and we need to respect her right to be silent.

WHEN YOUR FRIEND HAS A CRISIS
A crisis is a special sort of predicament. Most of the understandings and skills you need to help a friend out of a predicament are applicable also with a friend who is in a crisis. *But in addition to these,* you will need further abilities because of two special characteristics of crises—*size* and *urgency.* A crisis is a very large predicament that re-

---

Is Your Friend in a Crisis?

Place a check by the statements that apply to your friend.
_____ He or she has difficulty concentrating on what I say.
_____ He or she does not look at me when we talk together.
_____ He or she is not acting like his or her usual self.
_____ He or she is having difficulty getting along with close friends or family members.
_____ His or her productivity at work has dropped.

If you checked three or more statements, your friend may be experiencing a crisis. Read pages 25 to 32.

---

quires attention within a relatively short span of time. A crisis may be expected to last from one to six weeks. The *average* length of a crisis seems to be about two to three weeks.

RECOGNIZING A CRISIS

We often tend to be more aware of our own reactions than we are of other's actions. For this reason the following list of reactions is presented from *your* point of view as a friend and helper.

Remember that no one or two reactions serve as a sufficient indicator that your friend is in a state of crisis. There may be many other reasons for each of the following reactions. However, if you begin to get a pattern of a number of these reactions, then the possibility is increased that your friend may be undergoing a crisis.

1. *He's not listening to me.* You sense that you're not having a conversation. Your friend is not responding to you. He seems to have lost his ability to concentrate on a train of thought. Thus, a growing irritation inside you may be your first indicator that your friend is preoccupied by a crisis. It is important that you not be offended by your friend's temporary inability to listen to you; otherwise, you will be psychologically unavailable to help him when he needs you.

2. *He's not looking at me.* A person who is in the middle of a crisis may alternately look away from you as you talk with each

other and, at other times, may stare at you. In both cases your reaction is that his vision really stops inside his own head. He is caught up in his thoughts trying to figure out ways to extricate himself from his crisis, and he is attempting to avoid a sensory *overload*.

To understand the concept of overload think of a situation in which you were trying to find the answer to a problem, or remember a fact that keeps eluding you. At a time like this you may have closed your eyes to keep visual stimuli from overloading your circuits and interfering with your thought processes. In a situation in which a person wants to use all his mental energy to think of ways to get out of a crisis, he avoids an overload by looking at another person without really *seeing* him, and by looking at things that don't require mental processing. Many persons who are depressed or feeling down actually *look down,* that is, gaze at the floor.

3. *He doesn't act the way he usually does.* At this point, involvement as a *friend* pays off in helping. A stranger would not know whether a person's behavior is unusual or not, *for that person.* But *you* know if you have been acquainted with that person for some time. A quiet person may become talkative; a talkative person may rather suddenly come across as aloof or very quiet. You may observe a sudden change in eating habits or note unusual complaints about headaches or other bodily ailments.

4. *He isn't getting along with people close to him.* Freud said it was a sign of mental

health if we love and work well. The stress that goes with a crisis often interferes with our ability to continue a loving relationship with those close to us. If a person suddenly begins to treat his family and close friends badly, or without consideration, this may be an important clue to stress.

5. *He isn't getting his work done.* The ability to work well is the second sign of mental health mentioned in 4, above. Therefore, it is well to take into account a fairly abrupt decline in productivity.

One fall I noticed a student in one of my college classes rather abruptly (over a period of a week or two) stop producing. He not only did not do the required work, but he didn't appear to listen or to look at me when I was talking, or at other students when they were talking. His behavior was unusual in that he slouched and was very quiet, whereas he had formerly sat in an alert position and involved himself in the class activities. Also, he entered and left the classroom by himself instead of with other students, as he had formerly done. In other words, I reacted to him in each of the five ways.

After class one day when he was the last student to leave, I went over to him as he was getting his jacket on and his books together and said, "This has been a hard week for you." I said this in a way that let him know I understood that he was undergoing stress.

He looked at me as if he were deciding whether to trust me or not. Then he said,

"You want to know what I'm thinking about in this class and all my other classes!" I replied that I did, if he wanted to tell me. He then described his anguish as he sat through his classes thinking of his father, an alcoholic, who was operating a large combine daily, beginning the harvesting on the family farm. He finished by saying, "I wonder every day if today will be the day he kills himself on that combine."

After a time of talking, he decided to see his instructors and take a week out of school (he was so preoccupied he wasn't accomplishing anything anyway) and go home to run the combine for his father. He came back able to resume his work at college. He had made it through his crisis. Obviously, he would have other crises in the future, given his concern for his father.

THE FIRST HELPING STEPS

1. *Take time to be with your friend.* The first step in helping friends in a crisis is to just be *with* them. It means listening to the other person with as much concentration as you can muster.

A friend of mine told me yesterday that he went to visit a fellow employee of his who is dying with cancer. My friend said he couldn't think of anything to say, so he didn't say anything for ten minutes. He was just there in the room with the sick man. Then, they began to talk and they talked for two hours. It takes time to center one's attention on a person who is in a state of crisis.

2. *Expect that you will be able to help in some way.* If you begin to feel panicky yourself because you lack confidence, do some deep breathing while you are listening. This will aid you in relaxing. You will be able to help in most crisis situations if you focus on your friend's needs rather than your own. Count on your *presence* to make a positive difference.

3. *Establish eye contact with the person in crisis.* You cannot interact with your friend so long as he remains in a state of deep thought, fantasy, or daydream. Engage your friend visually. You may need to put a hand on his shoulder, say his name, or use another means of getting him to look at you and *see* you, but the eye contact is crucial. (If you are working with a visually impaired person, touch becomes even more important.) Sometimes it is useful to say to a person who seems to be looking right on through you, "I feel as though you are looking at me but not really seeing me."

4. *Bring your friend into the present.* Eye contact and touch help to move the other person out of his despair about the past or anxiety about the future. Some other means of doing this include listening to music, which is a present activity, or playing a game (whether it involves physical skills or is a simple table game), which requires concentration on a present task. Verbally echoing your friend's feelings will help him move into the present because emotions are "now."

5. *When necessary, discuss the way your friend talks.* Some persons in a crisis state increase their rate of speech until it is difficult to understand them. A response here could be, "I want to understand every word you are saying; please slow down so I can keep up with you." Others may slow their rate, mumble their words, or speak very softly. Request any necessary change, noting as above, that it is very important to you to understand what your friend is saying.

6. *Walk alongside your friend emotionally, rather than leaping ahead to find a "solution."* Remember that while problems have easy or satisfactory solutions, crises usually do not. What looks like a solution to a crisis from the viewpoint of an onlooker usually won't even make sense to the involved person. Your friend has to find his own ·vay, but he can find it better if you stay with him. If you "run ahead" looking for solutions, he may not be able to hear you.

7. *Accept your friend's point of view as being true for him, but be willing to state another point of view.* Pascal has said that when we wish to influence another person, we must be willing to grant the other person's point of view, and then suggest an additional point of view. We thus maintain the cordial relationship, while opening the person to a whole new way of looking at his situation.

An example of a helping response using this guideline could be, "I understand that you're feeling helpless right now, and I can

31

see you really are in a tough situation. Several times you have said, 'I can't do it.' Another way of looking at it is you could if you chose to. Could it be that it's more that you *won't* do it, rather than that you *can't* do it?"

You have to be involved with a person to say this, but if you *offer* it as an alternative rather than forcing it on him, he may gradually begin to buy the idea.

FOLLOW-UP

Because of the urgency and short-term nature of a crisis, follow-up becomes crucial. When you leave your friend it is important to ask him if he needs help in any other way, or if he has anyone to be with him. This is especially important at night when crises tend to seem overwhelming. A follow-up phone call in the evening will usually be appreciated.

As you make contact on a follow-up basis, look for emotional indicators that will let you know whether your friend is emerging from the crisis or moving into it. If the person is not able to resolve the crisis, he may panic. It is necessary that there be at least one person who says to the one who is in a state of crisis, "If you need me, just call me any time." Many times just knowing there is one person who is available enables the person to make it through the crisis.

[1]O. Hobart Mowrer, "Integrity Groups: Principles and Practices." *The Counseling Psychologist*, Vol. 3, No. 2, 1972, p. 22.

CHAPTER 2

How Predicaments Start

If you have determined that your friend's level of need is not urgent, you will have time to discover his strong and weak channels. Knowing your friend's strengths will enable you to build on them and knowing the weak channels will tell you what areas need to be improved.

Helping channels relate to the ways one typically responds to what one has learned. The channels I have found helpful to work with are *feeling* (awareness of one's emotions and the ability to express them); *thinking* (the ability to plan and the ability to connect cause and effect); *choosing* (establishing a clear set of values and moral standards, finding meaning in life, and having the courage or will to act). You need to know which channels are not functioning efficiently in order to help your friend become more "responseable"—that is, able to respond to his life fully through all three channels.

In the chart headed "Helping Channels" you will see three ways we *respond* to what

HELPING CHANNELS

CHANNEL	PERSON WITH STRONG CHANNEL	PERSON WITH WEAK CHANNEL	FORCES ENCOURAGING THESE CHANNELS
FEELING	Aware of own feelings; able to express them.	Doesn't know how to take own emotional pulse; may come across cold or inhibited.	Families, sharing groups, churches (especially where expression of feelings is fostered); coffee break talk.
THINKING	Analytical; investigative frame of mind.	Unaware; impulsive.	Schools, research institutes, games, e.g., chess.
CHOOSING	Courageous; has a clear value structure.	Indecisive.	Politics, religion, advertising.

we learn. If you are a person who is able to "image" well, imagine three small channels or tributaries flowing into a river. That river is your life. For most of us, these three channels would not be the same size. Usually we have a wide channel or two and a narrow channel. For example, a person who has a strong choosing channel tends to be courageous and to have a clear value structure. The person who has a constricted choosing channel is indecisive (1) because he lacks the courage to make a decision on insufficient evidences (and the evidences are always insufficient); or (2) because he does not have a value structure that is well organized. If all his values are equally important to him there is no way for him to prioritize in order to make a decision.

Now on this same chart notice over in the right column the forces that encourage one of these specific channels. Some churches, for example, appeal more to the feeling channel than do others. An example of a societal unity that focuses on thinking is the school. The school has typically seen children and youth as learning machines. Because of this, school administrators have sometimes overlooked the fact that students have feelings. Educators are beginning to work on various ways to fill this vacuum.

The richness of our lives is dependent on the free flow of each of our channels. To the extent that all of these channels are open and strong, our life is rich and fulfilling. But sometimes one of the channels is clogged.

One woman said concerning her husband, "I wish he'd just once say, 'I love you,' and put his arms around me when he didn't want sex." Her husband had so constricted his feeling channel that the expression of warmth didn't get through. This is not to say that he didn't love his wife, but warmth doesn't mean much *if it doesn't get through* to the other person.

WHY CRISES OCCUR

Let's suppose you have a friend who mentions to you that the right-hand tread on the front tires of his car is just about gone. At this point you could suggest he buy new front tires, or you could continue to listen. Let's suppose you continue to listen and he says his front tires have only ten thousand miles of wear on them. You now are relatively sure the front end of his car is out of line and this is causing the excessive tread wear. You talk with him about this possibility; it makes sense to him, and he decides to get his front wheels aligned.

It is important that your friend get new tires, but if he did not get the front wheels aligned, he would soon be back in the same old predicament of having unsafe front tires. In the same way, when your friend comes to you for help with some human predicament or crisis, it is almost never enough to help him "solve" the immediate problem. *It is usually the way we live that gets us into predicaments and crises*. Of course, this is

36

not always true. Sometimes there may be disease or an accident over which we have no control that can cause a crisis. But most of us would probably agree that we have gotten into the largest percentage of our jams under our own power.

It is usually the weak component of our life that gets us into a predicament. For example, one man lost the respect of his wife and that was his predicament. However, what he discovered he needed to work with was his weak choosing channel. He had gradually moved into a life-style that was marked by indecisiveness. Therefore, his wife had to make all the decisions regarding the children, the home, and sometimes even her husband. He had to discover this weak channel and strengthen it in order to get out of his predicament and to avoid similar ones in the future.

A LOOK AT YOU

As a helper, you cannot teach what you do not know. Therefore, you need to have worked through your own living channels in a careful way in order to determine your strengths and weaknesses, so that you can work on necessary growth. You need to learn how to determine your own strong and weak channels and the strong and weak channels of the friend who comes to you for help. It is most important that you be able to determine the *weak* channel, because this must be strengthened to get people out of present

WHAT ARE YOUR STRONG AND WEAK CHANNELS?

THE FEELING CHANNEL	THE THINKING CHANNEL	THE CHOOSING CHANNEL
___ 1. Someone has told you in the last six months that he/she appreciates your warmth.	___ 1. You usually consider consequences before acting.	___ 1. You make important decisions early and decisively, rather than spend a lot of time worrying about them.
___ 2. You usually are able to express angry feelings.	___ 2. You usually plan purchases well in advance and resist buying on impulse.	___ 2. You prefer to make your own decisions.
___ 3. You like to have people touch you.	___ 3. Once you've made plans you usually carry them out.	___ 3. You usually have a clear sense of what is right and wrong.
___ 4. You find it easy to touch people, especially those who are psychologically close to you.	___ 4. You are prompt for appointments.	___ 4. Life has a great deal of meaning for you.
___ 5. It is natural and easy for you to maintain eye contact with a person you are talking to.	___ 5. You can visualize the results of your actions easily.	___ 5. You have clear-cut personal goals.
___ 6. You enjoy receiving compliments and react graciously.	___ 6. You usually plan ahead and avoid predicaments.	___ 6. You can usually find the courage to make decisions you need to.
___ 7. You've been angry at	___ 7. When you have a task to	___ 7. You decide which

someone in the last few weeks.

____8. You've told someone within the last week that you appreciate, like, or love him/her.

____9. Others see you as a friendly person, easy to get to know.

____10. You smile as much, or more, than most people.

____11. You rarely use sarcasm.

____12. You often share your deep feelings with others.

Strong—*Warm;* very aware of emotions and effective in expressing them.

Weak—*Appears to be cold;* low in awareness and expression of emotions.

do, you typically do it rather than avoid it.

____8. You would classify yourself as dependable rather than undependable.

____9. It seems to be easier for you than for most to stay within a budget.

____10. At a restaurant you rarely order more than you can eat.

____11. You find it easy to think through your day tomorrow.

____12. You are strong in "sales resistance."

Strong—*A planner;* can visualize consequences of actions and can plan effectively.

Weak—*Impulsive;* has difficulty in planning ahead and in seeing consequences of action.

clothes you are going to wear each morning with little hesitation.

____8. You like to make moral decisions ahead of time rather than waiting until situations come up.

____9. Right now you're finding it fairly easy to decide which of these areas you're strong in.

____10. You could quickly and easily list three or four values in life that are very important to you.

____11. Courage ranks high in your value system.

____12. You feel confident of your decision-making ability.

Strong—*Decisive;* life is charged with meaning; has internalized moral standards, knows own values, demonstrates courage.

Weak—*Indecisive;* life may lack meaning, clear moral standards, a value system or courage.

crises and to enable them to avoid future ones.

I find I am sometimes unaware of some important things about me. We need to be reminded of the obvious. Most persons whom I have talked with do not know their strong and weak channels. Therefore, the accompanying chart can be helpful as a starting point. The checklist is set up in such a way that the column with the most checks indicates the strong channel and the column with the least checks indicates the weak channel.

Now take time to go through and put check marks to the left of each item that is typical of you. No one item means very much by itself, but taken all together you may find the results helpful. After you have finished the checklist, total the number of checks in each column. The column in which you have the least checks may be your weak channel. But don't make a firm decision on this yet. Think some more about it and, most important, talk with those closest to you about how they see you. The key at the bottom of the chart will help you understand your strong and weak characteristics.

Now that you have begun to establish what your weak channel is, you may wish to strengthen that channel. You will find in this section of the guide some approaches that are effective in strengthening each channel. Remember, it is the helpers who are working hardest at their own personal growth who are most helpful in reaching out to others.

You will find that it is no easy task to strengthen one of the channels because it will require you to make a change in the *way* you live.

A LOOK AT YOUR FRIEND

Having worked through the checklist and taken other steps to discover your channels, you now understand the concept well enough to use it with a friend. Also, having begun to strengthen your weak channel, you will realize how very difficult this is and that any help you give to your friend will have to go beyond pat answers and easy advice.

If your friend is in the predicament stage in terms of level of need, you can usually just give the checklist to him and ask him to fill it out. (Remember, we are taking for granted that your friend has come to you for help. It is not a workable thing to see somebody who needs help and try to give it to him if he does not want it. If he doesn't ask you in an outright way for help, at least there should be evidences that he wants help and is open to receiving it.) Just tell your friend that this is an important way to find out how he or she lives, that it helped you (if it did), and it would give the two of you something worthwhile to talk about.

CHAPTER 3

Helping an Inexpressive Friend

Let's suppose a friend comes to us for help, and we have concluded that this friend is weak in the feeling channel; that is, either he comes across as cold or he is unaware of some of the feelings he has, or both. There are some guidelines that will aid us in more effectively helping this friend.

ACCEPT, DON'T CONDEMN

Often the person who seems unable to get in touch with his feelings is not a cold or bitter person. He just comes across that way. Therefore, it is helpful to approach "cold" persons with the idea they are warm *inside*. If they come across as cold, usually they simply have not learned to express the warmth they have inside. This was true in my own life for many years. When I discovered that I often came across as cold, I began to work to express for others the warmth I felt for them.

We have a fireplace our family built. The chimney is made of an inner and outer tube of metal, with the two-inch circular space between packed with asbestos. Even when there is a roaring fire in the fireplace, the outside of the chimney is cool to the touch. It is possible that many people are so well insulated that the warmth inside doesn't get out to warm the person next to them.

It is good to accept the fact that most people have a good reason for being the way they are in terms of their coldness. For example, one middle-aged man went to see a counselor about several predicaments he was in. One of these predicaments was that the relationship between him and his daughter was a cold one. He wanted to show affection to her but he said he simply could not touch her or show her warmth. As this father continued to talk, he shared the information that in his own growing up days he had observed his father commit incest with his sister. Obviously, to him, physically touching or embracing his daughter would bring back many painful memories and would seem wrong.

This dad had to be taught through a series of task assignments to get closer to his daughter and to touch her and finally to get to the place where he would hug her, whether he felt like it or not. But the point is, if the counselor early in the sessions had mentally condemned the father as a person who didn't care about his daughter, then he would not have been able to help him. We have to accept people as they are in order to help them change.

If we have friends who are not in touch with their feelings, then it is probably best for us to assume that they have had experiences that have caused them to push their feelings down below the level of their awareness. It is not always necessary for us to know about these experiences. We just need to take the point of view that they have a good reason for doing what they're doing.

For example, a man who has difficulty sharing tender feelings with his wife may have been taught by others as he grew up that "macho" men only show toughness. If a person seems unable to share any of his angry feelings, it may be that the earlier expression of his angry feelings has resulted in someone hurting him physically or psychologically, or in leaving him. In other words, that person associates the expression of anger with the rejection or separation of a loved one.

SHARE YOUR WARMTH

Usually friends who come across as cold will begin to express their warmth to others, not when we have succeeded in "straightening them out," but rather when we have succeeded in *warming* them. We do this by being friendly to them and by investing our time with them. The friendliness must be genuine. One time a sixth grade teacher said to me, "I don't know what's wrong with that boy. I've tried everything with him; I've tried liking him." I suggested that if she had to

44

try to like him, he probably got the message.

It is possible to be involved in a "helping" relationship with another person whom we may not like. I remember teaching a senior class in high school and having one of the students tell me he didn't like me and that he wanted out of my class. I suggested he see one of the counselors in the school to obtain a transfer to another class. What disturbed me most when I looked at myself was that I had to admit I didn't like him and hadn't for some time. He saw a counselor who was a very wise person and who began to talk to him about my good points. I went to see the same counselor for help, and she began to talk to me about some of the things he had going for him. She also helped each of us to see some ways we needed to grow as persons. So we stayed together that year and by the end of the year we had begun to like each other.

"Cold" people are just like other people; they are looking for a warm place. You can provide that warm place as you spend time with your friend, affirm your friend as a person, and express your warmth.

GIVE STRAIGHT FEEDBACK
People usually don't change unless they see a reason to change. And our life-style is so much a part of us that our awareness of it is usually dim.

The approach of this manual takes for granted that you have built an involvement with your friend. This means that you can be direct with your friend and that you know him well enough, so that you know the best way to provide him or her information without hurting. For example, it may be helpful to say something like, "You seem to have a lot more warmth on the inside than you actually express to others." You should, of course, say this only if this judgment is true from your point of view.

If you're talking with a friend and he relates an incident that quite obviously makes him angry just to tell about it, you may wish to point out his anger. If he is weak in this feeling channel, he may deny the anger and say something like, "No, I'm not mad." Then if you have a good involvement, it is possible for you to mention physical evidence, such as, "Your face is flushed, your jaw is clenched, your forehead is wrinkled, the veins on your neck are standing out, and your fists are doubled up." You have to say this in the same way you would say, "Pass the salt." It will not work if you say it with an edge on your voice.

TOUCH THE BITTER PERSON
Sometimes people mention being out in "bitterly cold" weather. Just as cold weather is sometimes so sharp it is bitter, so bitterness in people sometimes goes with coldness, and is marked by intensity, regret, animosity, and unpleasantness. The bitter person is abrasive to anyone who happens

to be around, but most abrasive to people who are close. As a friend of mine says, "He is the kind of a person who would stroke a cat from the tail to the head."

The bitter person is often involved in predicaments and sometimes in crises. There is, of course, a tendency to upset and alienate others. The biggest predicament is the terribly heavy burden that bitter persons carry. It is a foul-smelling load from the past that they put on their shoulders again every morning—if they have been able to lay it down at night. Every day the load grows heavier because they are aware that they are hurting people every day unnecessarily. This has a ring of truth to most of us because at some time or other in our lives, we have personally known bitterness—our own. Perhaps someone reached out to help so it did not become a permanent part of our life-style.

The bitter person needs to learn how to forgive. I remember having a series of conversations with a very fine Christian businesswoman. She was middle-aged, competent, bright—and bitter. Her predicament was that she was alienating the persons around her, they were backing off, and loneliness was rapidly moving in. She was most bitter with her husband and with herself, but did not know how to shed the bitterness.

After trying many things that didn't work (helpers often experience failure!), I suggested she use a concordance and do a study of the word "mercy" as it occurs in the Bible.

(A concordance is a book that lists each time a word occurs in the Bible and gives the reference so that it can be looked up.)

We had two or three more conversations and then I didn't see her for nearly a year. She volunteered the information that this word study had helped her find forgiveness toward her husband and herself. She had studied many passages of Scripture over a period of months. One of these was Ephesians 2:4-7:

> But God, who is rich in mercy, out of the great love with which he loved us, even when we were dead through our trespasses, made us alive together with Christ (by grace you have been saved), and raised us up with him; and made us sit with him in the heavenly places in Christ Jesus, that in the coming ages he might show the immeasurable riches of his grace in kindness toward us in Christ Jesus.

Studying such references to mercy touched her life and she experienced again, in a time of renewal, the love of God, and was able to get rid of her bitterness.

Another way of touching a bitter person is through a spontaneous act of love or kindness. There are many examples of a child giving a hug to a cold, bitter man with the result that the "cold" person begins to melt. A neighbor brings in a cake to a cross, bitter woman next door and she begins to feel a strange warmth taking over inside.

Do You Need to Know Why?

Should you as a friend spend time helping someone discover why he feels or acts the way he does?

Most of us are tuned in to causes. Physicians spend time diagnosing the cause of an illness, believing that if they eliminate the cause of the illness, the illness will cease to exist. Psychiatrists, because they are physicians, typically use the same analytical approach. Usually this requires making the long trip back to the person's early childhood. This may be why psychiatrists, and some psychologists who use a similar analytical approach, are (unkindly) referred to as headshrinkers. They regress or "shrink" the person back to childhood.

There are some persons who are extremely disturbed who need to discuss their childhood in depth. A lay person should not attempt such analysis but should refer to a professional.

But for the great majority of people, it is not necessary, in order to change behavior and life-style, that either the person helping or the person being helped know *why* he is the way he is—for example, bitter. There are likely twenty-nine (or sixty-four) reasons. Nearly all behavior is *multiply* caused. It is usually a myth that one event in the distant past can be uncovered and the person is "OK" again. The truth is that most people turn their life-styles around, not by detective work, but by hard work and courage, and with some help from their friends.

STRENGTHEN THE FEELING CHANNEL

A person who is weak in his feeling channel is sometimes characterized by his lack of awareness of his own feelings. Just as some persons find it difficult to monitor their pulse rate by feeling their wrist at just the right place, so some find it difficult to get a reading on their emotional state. The person is thus placed at a great disadvantage. He may be showing his anger without even feeling it. The impact of this bent message will further confuse him. You can help your friend strengthen this important channel (feeling) by teaching him to monitor his "emotional pulse." What are some ways to do this?

1. *Use questions that teach, not corner, your friend.* Questions that may cause a friend to feel cornered include "Why did you feel that way?" and "Why did you do that?" Notice that both of these questions focus on the past. Questions that focus on the past typically are not very helpful. Also, questions that begin with why are usually not helpful. Most behaviors are multiply caused; that is, there are many causes for any single thing that we do. Therefore, most people cannot sort out all of these causes; and as a matter of fact, when they try to, they often miss some of the most significant causes.

Questions that tend to teach are open-ended questions such as "What are you doing about that?" "Is it helping?" and "How would you like to change?" These questions focus on present behavior for the most part. They are also goal-oriented rather than past-oriented. These kinds of questions will help get your friend to think about what he is *doing*. This is usually beneficial in bringing about change. Questions that help build an awareness of feelings include "What emotion are you feeling right now?" "Describe what you are feeling in your stomach (or chest)." "Where do you feel tension?" "Even though you're laughing right now, you seem angry to me. Are you *feeling* any anger?"

2. *Teach your friend to feel his/her body changes*. Just as we have to touch our body if we are going to take our pulse rate, so we

---

What Does Your Body Say?

Ask yourself the following questions.

- Is my forehead tightening or wrinkling?
- Are the muscles tensing around my eyes?
- Is the shape of my lower face changing so that my jaw is set and my teeth are clenched?
- Are my throat muscles tightening?
- Is there an acceleration in my pulse rate?
- Are my fists doubling up, or even slightly closing?
- Do I feel any tension across the upper and lower back?
- Is my breathing becoming more rapid?
- Is my stomach feeling tense, quivering, or "dis-eased"?
- Do my leg muscles feel taut?

If you answered yes to two or more of these questions, you may be experiencing some form of stress—anger, hurt, guilt, or disgust.

---

need to get in touch with our body if we are to be fully aware of our emotional changes. The secret to building awareness of our emotions is learning how to monitor the changes within our body. This takes some hard work. Most of us are not very aware of outer space, and are even less aware of "inner space."

When we experience negative emotions, we can see two trends in our body—a *speeding up* of the rhythms (circulation and breathing) and a *tightening up* of the muscles. The body is making preparations to fight or take flight.

3. *Pinpoint the negative emotion.* Once you teach your friend to monitor what is happening in his/her body in order to build awareness of negative emotions, the next step is to provide help in distinguishing the exact emotion. Two emotions that are very difficult to differentiate are anger and hurt. Some suggestions are given below that may help you work with your friend more effectively in these two areas.

To illustrate how these two emotions get mixed up, let's suppose that Roy, who is employed as an auto mechanic, goes to work and finds one of his fellow mechanics has been promoted to shop foreman. The manager of this particular dealership had told Roy two weeks ago that he was planning to name a new shop foreman and that Roy had an inside track on the job. Since that time Roy has had no further communication from the manager, so when he gets the news about the new foreman, Roy is upset—hurt. He is hurt because he did not get the job and because the manager did not talk with him to explain why the implicit promise was broken.

THE INTERACTION OF HURT, ANGER, AND REVENGEFULNESS

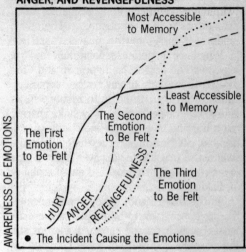

(From *Family Problems and Predicaments* by Paul Welter, Tyndale House, 1977.)

Notice on the drawing "The Interaction of Hurt, Anger, and Revengefulness" that seconds after the event that arouses the hurt feeling, another feeling skyrockets into awareness—anger. This overlays the hurt feeling so that Roy is no longer aware of his new emotion. A bit later he may begin to want to "get back at" the manager. This new emotion—revengefulness—can trigger

53

some negative action if Roy does not keep it under control.

Another point of the drawing is that later when Roy thinks about the event that hurt him, he moves back into his memory and encounters the *last* emotion first. Therefore, instead of going to the manager and explaining his hurt and disappointment that the manager had gotten his hopes up and then dashed them without any further communication, Roy is more likely to respond in an angry way, or perhaps he may sulk. Sharing one's hurt feelings keeps one open and vulnerable. Sharing angry or revengeful feelings (when the original feeling was hurt) keeps one closed and may close off any possibility of dialogue.

On the other hand, if Roy communicates his anger effectively by pinpointing *exactly* what it was that made him mad, there is still the possibility of getting some communication going. If he reacts angrily without discussing the real issue, then there is little chance of resolving the issue. The point is that we communicate most clearly when we talk with another person about the *first* emotion we felt in the interaction between us.

I work in a college, and sometimes I see girls and guys who respond to each other angrily or in a revengeful way when the original separating emotion between them was hurt. When they choose to hurt back instead of communicating the fact that they were hurt, they further widen the psychological distance between them.

If your friend is caught in this predicament, you may be able to help him/her get back to the original emotion and *feel* the hurt. This will take some doing, because it is hard to get beneath the anger. Often when people move back beyond anger to their hurt, they sigh and relax, and the tension leaves, just like the air going out of a balloon. Then they are usually able to go to the other person and discuss this hurt.

4. *Teach your friend to monitor his/her actions.* In order to take our emotional pulse it is helpful not only to monitor what is happening in our bodies, but also the actions we are taking. For example, if we become aware that we are yelling, this tells us that we do not believe we are being heard. Probably we are feeling frustrated, perhaps angry. If this happens, it is usually effective to stop yelling and say something like, "I don't know if this is the way it really is, but I have the feeling you aren't listening to me right now."

If we become aware we are backing up, even very slightly, in a discussion with another person, it usually means we want to get out of the situation. We may be afraid or tired, or for some other reason want to terminate the conversation. It is helpful at this point to try to discover what is happening that is causing us to retreat, and to talk about that.

It is important to monitor the way we are talking. If we discover we are talking in a cutting way, this means that we want to hurt the other person. At this point, integrity would require that we apologize to the other person and discuss what is between us. This requires a considerable amount of both humility and courage.

5. *Teach your friend to monitor the other person's reactions.* This can be done with the same guidelines mentioned above for monitoring our own actions. If the other person raises his/her voice, then we need to say something like, "I'm noticing you are now talking quite loudly; do you feel I'm not listening to you?" If the other person backs away from us, we need to ask ourselves if we are coming across as attacking. We can learn a great deal about our own emotions by becoming aware of what the other person is doing in reaction to us.

The above guidelines for teaching your friend to take his/her emotional pulse are based on the view that you have a close, warm relationship with your friend and that your friend is seeking help. This provides the openness, trust, and motivation to allow these guidelines to work.

CHAPTER 4

Helping an Impulsive Friend

The person who is weak in the thinking channel is typically an impulsive person. As you will notice from the drawing, the impulsive person goes directly from feeling to doing without moving through the thinking and choosing channels. If it looks good, he buys it. If it tastes good, he eats it. If it feels good, he does it. He is a creature of his feelings, and to the extent that he is controlled only by his feelings he goes through life "out of control."

THE BYPASS

FEELING
THINKING
CHOOSING
DOING

Using the framework of the four ancient temperaments—sanguine, melancholic, choleric, and phlegmatic—the impulsive person fits rather well the typical description of the sanguine. O. Hallesby has shown in his very helpful book *Temperament and the Christian Faith* that the sanguine has many strengths. [1] The sanguine, like a child, lives in the present. He therefore can enjoy life and can interact in a warm, effective way with others. But there are weaknesses as well. He usually leaves unfinished many tasks he has begun. He has good intentions, but he often forgets these intentions and his problems. Because he is a child of the moment, he is not easily able to visualize outcomes of his actions. He is open to his senses, but to some extent they control him.

> As a butterfly flutters from one flower to another, so his impressionable mind flutters from one sensation to another. He enjoys them all as long as they last, but when they're driven away by new impressions, he is through with them. [2]

SLOW DOWN THE IMPULSIVE PERSON

How can you go about slowing down the impulsive person? If you are standing near a large slippery slide and you see a little child going down the slide at such a high rate of speed that you are sure there is some danger involved, the only way you can slow him down is to get very much involved with

about that for awhile and then told him I didn't have a "dumped-on" feeling because I learned something from every person I worked with. Then I told him the things I had learned from him and his wife. They were both surprised they had helped me. They had been much more aware of their weaknesses than their strengths.

3. *Explain the way you help.* Your friend will likely come to you for help, as most impulsive persons do, when he has gotten himself into some predicament because of his shortsightedness. You need to do what you can to help your friend out of that immediate predicament. Then you need to clarify the way you can be most helpful.

One way is by pointing out to your friend that you have observed that he sometimes makes decisions without thinking where these decisions will land him, much in the same way one might jump off the platform of a slippery slide onto the slide without looking at the bottom of the slide to see whether it has a hard or soft landing. Let your friend know that you feel you can be of help to him if he will talk with you about the decision he is planning to make. He will still have the responsibility for those decisions, because you won't tell him what to do. However, just talking about the decision may help him to get a better understanding of the outcomes and consequences that he is committed to by making the decision.

4. *Ask for a commitment to change.* When your impulsive friend comes to you and asks

for help, and you help in whatever way you can to assist him in the immediate predicament, then there is another important step. You need to ask him if this way of living is working for him—that is, making impulsive decisions and finding the landings are hard.

If he says that he wants to change and wants to think through the outcomes prior to taking actions, then you will need to point out that it will take very hard work. Sometimes a statement such as, "This may be the hardest work you have ever done," is helpful in letting impulsive persons count the cost. Otherwise, it is possible for them to embark on this venture in the same light-hearted impulsive fashion in which they begin other ventures. So questions such as, "Are you sure you want to work at this?" may serve to secure an oral contract that will increase perseverance. And if your friend replies, "No, I'm not sure," then don't push for a commitment. He has to be *ready* to change before he can successfully bring about this move away from impulsiveness.

5. *Do not accept irresponsible statements and actions.* The impulsive person tends to blame circumstances or other people for his unwelcome predicaments. He sometimes sees bad outcomes as just "happening." Sometimes he may blame them on fate. Sometimes he may blame them on God.

If from your point of view the consequences are very natural, based on his actions, it is important to provide him with this information. This needs to be done, not in a blaming way or with an edge on your voice. Rather, you need to point out in a matter-of-fact, natural way that it seems clear enough to you why the action he took got him into the predicament he is in now. And you need to line these out in a chronological, cause-effect way. Remember that the impulsive person often fails to connect cause and effect, so you need to review consequences with him from time to time.

6. *Provide encouragement.* The impulsive person is easily discouraged. He can go all the way from full speed ahead to a grinding halt in a few moments' time. Therefore, at times he will need help in slowing down his out-of-control, careening life; at other times he will need help starting up again when he has crashed head-on with a predicament or crisis. Remember that encouragement means your friend gains *courage* from being with you. He's then willing to go at it again and take risks when necessary to reach his goal. He will draw courage from your presence and from your affirming him as a person.

TEACH YOUR FRIEND TO PLAN AHEAD

My weakest channel in my growing-up days was in the area of thinking. My first year in college I worked as a houseboy in a sorority, and for that effort I received my meals and $10 a month. I applied the $10 to the rent for a room where I was living. With the little money I had saved I could just barely get by.

One day I was downtown and saw a ballpoint pen that I liked. Ballpoint pens cost more then and this was a very good one. In fact, it cost $12.50. I impulsively bought that pen and then spent the rest of the month wondering, "Why did I do that?"

I was the youngest in our family and it is my observation that the youngest member of a family is a bit more likely to be impulsive and to fail to plan ahead. The youngest member of the family, more than the other children, expects people to do things for him because he grows up surrounded by older, bigger, and more able people. At any rate, it seemed to me I had to work harder than most to reach the point where I was taking the initiative and planning ahead.

Two Ways to Think Ahead

1	If I do this, X ————→ X CAUSE	then this will happen. EFFECT
2	then I need to make this plan. X ←———— X PLAN	If I want to reach this goal X GOAL

The person who is strong in the thinking channel is able to do two things well. He can go from cause to effect and visualize what the *outcomes* of his actions will be. He can also think backward from a goal to a *plan* for reaching that goal. These two efforts require thinking in both directions—forward and backward. The person who is weak in the thinking channel is weak in both of these. It is helpful to encourage him to state a goal and then to think back toward the present in establishing a plan. The following guidelines have been beneficial in doing this.

1. *Ask "Tell me your dream."* The impulsive person needs a strong enough goal in the future to motivate him to plan carefully to reach that goal. One of the questions I ask persons who come to me for help is some form of the question, "What do you want out of life?" Another way of putting it is "What kind of life do you want?" or "Would you be willing to share your dream with me?" I did this just last week with a graduate student who replied, "Yes, I'll share my dream, and it's something I've only shared with two or three other people." Then he went on to share the kind of life he wanted ten years from now. You may have to phrase the question in several different ways, but the chances are you'll get an answer, because most people want a chance to share their dream.

2. *Ask "What is your plan?"* William Glasser has written in a helpful way concerning the value of asking for a plan. He tells of his counseling sessions with a young man who wanted to recount his failures of the past in great detail.

Instead I took the initiative. I asked him to tell me his plans (a favorite Reality Therapy question). Asking him for his plan tells him that he should have a plan, or at least start thinking of one, putting him in a position where, instead of unburdening his troubles, he should begin some constructive thinking about what he is doing right now and about his future. He reacted typically by asking, "What plan, what do you have in mind?" I said, "Well, here you are at college. You must have a plan, or a goal, some place you are heading for, some idea of how to get there."[3]

A plan is the bridge that connects the dream to the reality. Now there is something romantic-sounding and attractive about a dream. And the achievement of that dream is very attractive. But a plan? A plan sounds less attractive, somewhat tedious, humdrum, and not particularly interesting. But a plan is what makes it all possible. And it need not be boring. There is nearly always adventure between a dream and the achievement of that dream. The purpose of a plan is to make the adventure successful.

THE BRIDGE

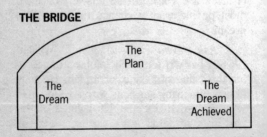

3. *Help him set up a plan.* To set up an effective plan, your friend will need your help to visualize his dream as specifically as possible. He will need to "image" the hoped-for outcome as fully and sharply as possible.

For example, let's suppose you have a friend who, although he has many fine characteristics, is quite impulsive. He is twenty-three years old, married, and has one child, loves cars, and is deeply in debt. Both he and his wife have steady jobs, but periodically he buys a car on impulse, or buys sports accessories for his car. He comes to you for help because his marriage is getting shaky. His wife has told him to "grow up" and to use his money for rent and groceries.

During the conversation you ask him what it is he wants out of life—what his dream is. He may reply that he hasn't thought about this, or he may say, "I'd really like to have this neat Corvette I saw the other day!" You realize you have a tough one on your hands.

You may have to shock him to do some serious thinking with a reply such as, "I can't help you if your goal in life is just to get a different kind of machine. What kind of *life* do you want? Are you satisfied with your relationship with your wife and child?"

If he still talks about cars, you may need to tell him that it sounds as if he is not ready to make a change yet. If he does talk about wanting to get along better with his wife or having her get along better with him, try to get him to specify what this would mean. Suppose he says, "Well, for one thing, it would mean she would stop nagging me about money all the time." Now you have something specific to go on, and you can reply, "What is your plan for changing the way you do things so that you eventually will have enough money to meet the needs for your family?" The plan may include the idea that each partner in the marriage be given veto power over any expenditure twenty-five dollars and higher. It may include putting a small amount in savings each month or agreeing to visit with a financial counselor. Loan officers in banks and credit unions are excellent sources for professional financial advice. You will need to help your friend establish a time line by asking questions such as: "When would you like to be out of debt?" or "How long do you think it will take you to have enough money each month to meet your household needs?"

Another question worth asking is "How far on the way to your dream do you want to be one year from now?" Or, for a very impulsive person who can't think that far ahead, ". . . six months (or one month) from now?" Thinking through the answer to this question enables your friend to move backward toward the present and begin to think more concretely in terms of the initiative he is going to need to take.

4. *Help him follow through.* Questions like the following can help provide determination: "This plan is going to take a lot of work. Are things bad enough that you're willing to put out the necessary time and energy to im-

prove them in this way?" "Is this plan realistic—is it going to be possible for you to carry it out?" At this point some will say they don't want to do it or they don't think they can. It is important not to urge them because they will not succeed if they don't think they can make it.

Another question that may prove beneficial is "What do you need to be doing now in order to proceed toward your goal?" The identification of this first step is extremely important. It should be clear and specific enough so that your friend knows when it is done. Finishing the first step is a strong reinforcer.

Another question is "From whom do you need help?" This tells your friend he need not be alone in his plan and venture. As a friend you are in a good position to make other helping persons and agencies available.

[1] O. Hallesby, *Temperament and the Christian Faith* (Minneapolis, Minn.: Augsburg Publishing House, 1962).

[2] Ibid., p. 23.

[3] William Glasser, *Reality Therapy* (New York: Harper Colophon Books, Harper and Row, 1965), p. 37.

Helping an Indecisive Friend

An important guideline used in this manual is that we must be *with* a person before we can do anything *for* that person. Being with your friend means that you listen desperately to what your friend is saying. You make no attempt to give any pat answers or easy solutions or advice. Being with your friend requires that you listen in such a way and respond in an accurate enough manner that your friend knows that he is being deeply understood. After you have worked through this first state of being with your friend and hearing him out, usually he will begin to want to move toward some kind of action.

Based on what you know about your friend, you may have already concluded that he or she is weak in the choosing channel. You also may have shared the "Checklist for Discovering Strong and Weak Channels" with him or her.

PINPOINT THE SOURCE
OF INDECISION

Once you have determined that your friend is weak in the choosing channel, you need to decide which of the three areas—meaning, values, or moral standards—is the weakest. Although these areas overlap each other, the checklist will enable you to make a good guess about the weakest area of the choosing channel. Items 1, 2, 4, 6, 11, and 12 of the checklist have to do with meaning. Items 3 and 8, if not checked, indicate that there may not be a well-developed set of moral standards. Items 5 and 10 relate to values.

While establishing the area of the choosing channel that your friend needs help in, you can help him or her get out of the *immediate* predicament. A helpful guideline here is that your friend usually will find the way out of the immediate predicament by finding the *courage* to make the decision that needs to be made. It will be important for you to talk with your friend about how *the way we are living* may involve us in predicaments. To avoid future predicaments we need to consider *changing* the way we live. When your friend has made some progress in getting out of his or her immediate predicament, you are ready to begin helping with a lifestyle change. It is important not to wait until the person has gotten completely out of the predicament, or else the motivation to change may be decreased.

CHALLENGE NATURAL CHARACTERISTICS

There are several characteristics of indecisive persons that require one to relate with them in a special way. Traits that go with indecision include worry, dependence, and wavering (second-guessing oneself).

1. *Worry.* It isn't worth trying to figure out whether indecision causes one to worry, or whether worry causes one to be indecisive. Probably there is a circular effect. At any rate, the indecisive person is usually worried, sometimes edgy, and on occasion panicky.

So what does this mean for the person who is trying to help? Well, for one thing it means that it doesn't work to say to the indecisive person, "Don't worry about it," because that just gives him one more thing to worry about. In fact, this particular admonition is not an effective one to give anybody. It's like ordering someone to stop crying.

We need to have peace and confidence in our own life. The worried person draws calm, not from our advice, but from us—from our *presence.* Can you think now of a time when you were worried, and the calming effect that the presence of a strong, peaceful person had on you? You can provide that presence for a person who comes to you for help.

2. *Dependence.* The indecisive person is usually excessively dependent on others for decision-making. He likes (and also

sometimes resents) others' help in making choices. Looking back, I can see this characteristic in my own life.

When I was about twenty or twenty-one, I frequently went to see the Rev. Henry Weinberg, a retired seventy-five-year-old minister. I thought it was "just to talk." Really, it was to get him to help me with decisions I needed to make. Finally, one time after Henry (he preferred "Henry" to "Rev. Weinberg") had sensed that I wanted him to take the responsibility for my decisions, he said, "Paul, I'm glad to talk with you, but you have to make your own decision. I have enough responsibility just making the decisions I have to make." That straightforward statement, said in a gentle way, put some steel into me. I found it more possible to make decisions after that.

So what I learned about helping from Henry was to open myself to talk with others about the decision they needed to make, but not to take away that important responsibility of *making* the choice. This requires considerable strength and insight, because some persons push hard and subtly. The ones who push the hardest are the ones who are the most frightened of making a decision all by themselves.

3. *Wavering (second-guessing oneself).* The indecisive person fits the description of the doubter, given in James 1:6-8: "He who doubts is like a wave of the sea that is driven and tossed by the wind . . . a double-minded man, unstable in all his ways."

The ambivalent person leans one direction, then a new piece of information arrives and he leans the other. The reason he is leaning all the time is that he doesn't step out, he doesn't commit himself in either direction; so since he doesn't move, he just leans.

The wavering person is thus characterized by a lack of commitment. Are there special ways of working with persons who lack this characteristic?

First, you may expect his call for help to be uncertain. He may come to you asking for help in some predicament, and may even want help in strengthening his choosing channel. The next day or next week he may have changed his mind. Knowing this in advance will help you accept him in his changeableness. Also it may keep you from taking it personally if he seems at first to want your help and then rejects it. You will understand that this changed attitude is more likely a function of his second-guessing himself than of anything you have done.

The most difficult aspect of working with this person is to get him to decide exactly what he wants to change and to follow through on his plan for change. Decisions and stick-to-itiveness come hard to the second-guesser. So what does this mean to you? It means that your friend needs to encounter in you a person who does not waver back and forth and who is strong enough to lean on—for support, not decision. Have you ever leaned on a post that was not fairly embedded in the ground? The harder you lean, the less support it gives. We need to provide a steadying influence.

You can also ask questions if your friend begins working on a plan and then changes his mind, such as: "You chose to do this and now you've changed your mind. What new evidences caused you to make a different decision?" "Do you think that reversing your decision could be an example of the indecisiveness you are wanting to change?" It is important that the tone of such questions be matter-of-fact rather than persuasive. He needs to learn to make his decisions on solid information rather than because people are pushing him.

4. *Lack of basis for decision making.* A person who lacks meaning in life does not have a basis for making important decisions. The decision to continue living is based on courage. One person called me at night and said, "I have a bottle of sleeping pills in my hand and I'm thinking of committing suicide. I almost had the courage to do it awhile ago and then I chickened out."

After I thought a bit, I reminded the caller that it did not require courage to take the bottle of sleeping pills; it took courage to make the decision *not* to take the pills—to keep on living even when life seemed to have no meaning. At this point we began to build an involvement and he was willing to start a deeper search for meaning.

The same element—discouragement— that offers a clue that meaning is lacking in a person's life also provides a starting point in helping your friend. What do you do with a discouraged person? You encourage him. A person who is discouraged lacks courage. To encourage someone is to provide him with courage. How is this done?

ENCOURAGE YOUR FRIEND

It is helpful to take a look at what encouragement is *not*. Encouragement is not urging. Sometimes we may use the word *encourage* when we mean *urge*, as in the sentence, "I encouraged him to make the decision." Urging is rarely helpful. The reason for this is that it almost always creates resistance. As noted earlier, if you have had anybody come up behind you and push you with his hands against your back, you have noticed that your usual reaction is to dig your heels in and stay put. Psychological pushing usually accomplishes the same result.

Encouragement is not reassurance. Reassurance is an attempt to make someone feel better by telling him "Things are OK" or "Things will turn out OK." Reassurance is generally not helpful and can actually be harmful. If we tell somebody that things are OK when they're not OK, this only tends to confuse the other person. If we try to predict the future and tell that person things will turn out OK and in fact, they turn out badly, this may tend to disillusion the other person and decrease the involvement between the two of us.

Let's suppose a high school friend has just confided in you what she would like to tell her parents in order to have a better relationship with them. A reply using the urging method might be "I think you should talk to them. Why don't you do it tonight?" A reply using the reassurance technique might be "I'm sure if you would talk to them, they wouldn't get mad at you." An encouraging reply might be "I can see you have the courage to sit down and talk with your parents just as you did with me."

Encouragement does not minimize the risk involved in an action. An encouraging remark might be "I can see that would be a risky thing to do. Could you find the courage to give it a try?"

It is helpful in giving encouragement to point out the double risk that is inherent in most situations. For example, if you are talking to a good friend and he tells you that he has worked at the same place for some time without a raise but he is afraid to talk to his boss, it may be helpful to reply in a way similar to this: "It sounds as though you're afraid to run the risk of losing your job if you ask your boss for a raise; on the other hand, if you don't, is it possible that you run the risk of continuing to build up resentment and putting yourself down for not taking actions?"

We must know our friend well enough to know what kind of remark would be encouraging and what kind would be discouraging. Remember that any two people may

77

react in exactly opposite ways. The essential thing is to find the approach that will enable our friend to face the risks squarely.

DETECT A SENSE OF FAILURE

Many people feel as though they are failures and that therefore life lacks meaning. It is rarely helpful to try to convince a friend that he is not a failure when he feels as though he is. It is more effective to make a statement such as the following: "I can understand from your point of view that you see yourself as a failure," and then take the following two steps:

1. Ask a question such as, "All right, so you see yourself as a failure; if you became a successful person, would life be full of meaning for you?" Then introduce Victor Frankl's diagram showing the relationship between failure and success, and despair and meaning.

Frankl saw the line running from failure to success as being in a different plane altogether than the line running from despair to meaning. Therefore, just because one would see himself as farther right on the line (that is, would identify himself as a successful person), this would not necessarily mean that he would be any higher on the vertical line (that is, regard his life as being more filled with meaning). A simple diagram like this that you can draw on a napkin when you are having coffee, for example, often provides your friend with an image that he can remember.

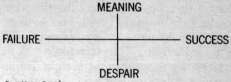

2. If your friend sees himself as a failure, and if you have a strong involvement with him, you may wish to ask the question, "What is your plan for becoming successful?" Often the answer comes out rather vague, because the person who has built a failure pattern typically lacks concreteness. You may use further questions to help your friend become more and more concrete. These questions may include, "Yes, but what will be your first step?" and "What is one activity you could do today or tomorrow that would move you toward becoming successful?"

MY OWN SEARCH FOR MEANING
I don't know for sure how it is for others in their quest for meaning, but I know in my own search there were three factors involved. First there was a need for *identity*. I needed to know who I was. Then there was a need for a *relationship*. I needed a sense of belonging. The third thing I was looking for was a *cause*. I needed to belong not only to a person but to a cause.

In the midst of my own search, a newly

found friend shared with me the meaning that coming to know Jesus Christ had for him. I then began to study the Bible and particularly the life of Christ. I began to understand why Jesus had come to earth and had lived and died. The resurrection took on a brand new meaning to me. In short, I made a personal decision for Christ. After the decision, I began to find my *identity* as a member of the family of God. I saw myself as having been created in the image of God and redeemed by Jesus. And while I perceived creation and redemption as being an experience I held in common with others, I realized that God was not a rubber-stamp Creator, and that I was as unique as my fingerprints. My identity thus became increasingly clear to me.

The second part of my search, the quest for a *relationship*, was fulfilled by me entering into this relationship with God and into a fellowship of persons I began to see as my brothers and sisters. As Dr. Robert Manley, a Nebraska historian, has pointed out, the most important community is not a geographical community but a community of those with similar values and beliefs.

The third aspect of my search for meaning was a *cause*. I found this cause to be sharing the message and the love of Jesus Christ.

YOUR SEARCH FOR MEANING
If you have been deeply involved in your own search for meaning, then you are in a position

to assist another person with his or her search for meaning. However, if you have been so busy with day-to-day living that you have not entered into a deep search for what life is all about, for your own identity, for a significant relationship and a cause, then it is doubtful if you can help another person with such a search. We cannot give what we do not have. If someone comes to us for help in the search for meaning, and we have not been involved deeply in this search of ourselves, then we should do what we need to do in any helping area in which we lack confidence or skills. In such a case we need to refer the person to someone else who can help.

[1]Victor E. Frankl, *Psychotherapy and Existentialism: Selected Papers on Logotherapy* (New York: Simon and Schuster, 1967), p. 27.

Questions to Ask a Friend

Daily Meaning. I have sometimes found it helpful to ask those involved in a quest for meaning about the activities that have a meaning for them right now. These would include such questions as the following:

1. What have you done today that has had the most meaning for you?
2. What relationship has the most meaning for you?
3. What meaning does your job have for you?
4. What do you do when you don't have to do anything?

Personal Goals. The following questions about goals need to be asked in a matter-of-fact way, with goodwill, and with no intent to corner the person. Rather, the intent should be to teach. Questions may include ones similar to the following:

1. From your point of view, what seems enough to live for?
2. What do you expect will be most important in your life five years from now?
3. If you had what you really wanted in life, what would you have?
4. What future goal, if you could achieve it, would result in your life being filled with meaning?
5. What is your dream?

Learning Channels

In order to help a friend, you need to discover his preferred style of learning. By learning style, I mean one's method of bringing in new information most efficiently and making sense of it. Right now you are using a visual method as you read this line of print. If this information were on a cassette, you would be using your hearing channel. Some persons learn more efficiently by seeing, some by hearing, and some by touch or movement.

We can make our helping more effective if we can find out how our friend learns best. For example, a young woman came for help because her marriage was not as fulfilling as she expected and wanted it to be. Through observation and some methods to be discussed later, I decided that Beth was a visual learner (this was her strong learning channel).

She liked to read and to summarize her reading by writing notes. At this point I knew it would be helpful to use written matter in addition to the regular talk-listen approach

LEARNING CHANNELS

CHANNEL	SOME WAYS IN WHICH INFORMATION IS RECEIVED THROUGH THIS CHANNEL	BASIC HELPER STRATEGIES
HEARING	Listening to words, listening to other sounds	Talk, listen, use a cassette tape, play music
SEEING	Reading, looking at others, viewing TV	Show, use illustrated or printed material, use other visual aids
TOUCHING/ MOVING	Touching, getting "feedback" from joints and muscles	Touch, use gestures, roleplays, task agreements

of a counseling session. Each time I saw her, I loaned her a book or article to read. She also loaned me two or three books of hers to read (visual learners like to loan books). I found these books helpful, and we were able to spend some useful time discussing the books we had both read. From these books, and from our discussion of them, she was able to apply several new ideas to help improve her relationship with her husband.

Notice the following diagram on "Learning Channels." There are a number of learning channels, but three primary ones. The hearing and seeing channels are well known, but the touch/movement learning channel is less well known. This channel includes the sense of touch (tactile) and the sensory input that comes from the movement of joints, muscles, and limbs (kinesthetic). Examples of touch/movement learning would be sensing with one's fingers where to hold an egg when breaking it, or learning something about another person through a handshake.

DISCOVER YOUR LEARNING CHANNEL
All of us, unless we have a sensory impairment such as blindness or deafness, use all three of these channels—as well as others, such as the sense of smell. Most people can identify a channel that is strongest. However, there are some persons who seem to learn equally well through all three of the major channels. It is important to keep in mind that we are not talking about the *only* way

WHAT'S YOUR LEARNING CHANNEL?

STRONG IN VISUAL CHANNEL	STRONG IN AUDITORY CHANNEL	STRONG IN TOUCH/ MOVEMENT CHANNEL
___ 1. Likes to keep written records	___ 1. Prefers to have someone else read instructions when putting a model together	___ 1. Likes to build things
___ 2. Typically reads billboards while driving or riding	___ 2. Reviews for a test by reading notes aloud or by talking with others	___ 2. Uses sense of touch to put a model together
___ 3. Puts model together correctly using written directions	___ 3. Expresses self best by talking	___ 3. Can distinguish items by touch when blindfolded
___ 4. Follows written recipes easily when cooking	___ 4. Talks aloud when working a math problem	___ 4. Learns touch system rapidly in typing
___ 5. Reviews for a test by writing a summary	___ 5. Prefers listening to a cassette over reading the same material	___ 5. Gestures are a very important part of communication
___ 6. Expresses self best by writing	___ 6. Commits Zip Code to memory by saying it	___ 6. Moves with music
___ 7. Writes on napkins in a restaurant	___ 7. Uses rhyming words to remember names	___ 7. Doodles and draws on any available paper
___ 8. Can put a bicycle together from a mail order house	___ 8. Calls on the telephone to compliment a friend	___ 8. An "out-of-doors" person

86

using only the written directions provided

___ 9. Commits a Zip Code to memory by writing it

___ 10. Uses visual images to remember names

___ 11. A "bookworm"

___ 12. Writes a note to compliment a friend

___ 13. Plans the upcoming week by making a list

___ 14. Prefers written directions from employer

___ 15. Prefers to get a map and find own way in a strange city

___ 16. Prefers reading/writing games like "Scrabble"

___ 9. Plans the upcoming week by talking it through with someone

___ 10. Talks to self

___ 11. Prefers oral directions from employer

___ 12. Likes to stop at a service station for directions in a strange city

___ 13. Prefers talking/listening games

___ 14. Keeps up on news by listening to the radio

___ 15. Able to concentrate deeply on what another person is saying

___ 16. Uses "free" time for talking with others

___ 9. Likes to express self through painting or dance

___ 10. Moves easily; well coordinated

___ 11. Spends a large amount of time on crafts and handwork

___ 12. Likes to feel texture of drapes and furniture

___ 13. Prefers movement games to games where one just sits (this may also be a function of age)

___ 14. Finds it fairly easy to "keep fit" physically

___ 15. One of the fastest in a group to learn a new physical skill.

___ 16. Uses "free" time for physical activities

(From *Family Problems and Predicaments*, by Paul Welter, Tyndale House, 1977.)

a person learns, but rather that person's *most efficient* learning channel.

Look at the accompanying chart and note that there is a place to check the items that are most descriptive of you. You will find that this is a difficult task because, if you are like most persons, it is something you have not thought much about. Using a pencil (because you may wish to erase and mark a different item), place a check mark in front of each item that would usually be descriptive of you. If there is an item you cannot decide on, even after you have reflected on it for some time, ask another person in your family or a close friend how he/she would mark it for you. For example, a close friend might be able to note whether you should check "Expresses self best by talking" or "Expresses self best by writing" as a more accurate description of you.

After you have finished, look at the results. Remember that no single item by itself will tell you your learning style. Rather you need to look for a pattern. You may find that you have about the same number of check marks in each column. If you do, then you will probably draw the tentative conclusion that you learn about equally well with each channel.

However, it is somewhat more likely that you will find as you look at the completed page that the number of marks in one column will "stand out" over the number of marks in the other two columns. If that is the case, then you may draw the tentative conclusion that you are probably strong in that particular channel. A very low number of marks in one of the columns may indicate that that is your least used, or least efficient, or a "weak," learning channel. Make sure at this point that your conclusions are only tentative ones. You should leave room for changing your mind about your strong channel as you gather more information about the way you learn.

After you understand how to use the checklist, you can ask your friend to take it himself.

HELP YOUR FRIEND LEARN

If a friend comes to you for help, you will be able to provide that help in the most effective way if you know how your friend learns. People need to receive help in their own special way. Part of that special way has to do with their strong learning channel.

Let's suppose that you have a friend who has an alcoholic husband. If your friend has a strong visual channel then you may choose to leave some *printed materials* on Alcoholics Anonymous. On the other hand, if she is an auditory learner, you may wish to *talk* with her about the resources of Alcoholics Anonymous.

If it isn't appropriate to use a checklist with your friend, or if you have used it and still are not sure which is your friend's strong learning channel, finding answers to some of the questions below may aid you in helping your friend discover his strong learning channel.

1. How much time does your friend spend reading, in comparison to time spent in listening to the radio or to music? This often provides a clue to your friend's strong learning channel.

2. Does your friend talk with you about new things he has *read* or new things he has *heard*? The answer to this question will tell you how your friend typically acquires new information.

3. What does your friend do when he does not have to do anything? In that activity, which of the three learning channels is most involved—visual, auditory, or touch/movement?

4. How does your friend memorize names and numbers? This requires careful observational skills. People memorize in many different ways. There is a person in the city in which I live who has perfect pitch. Having perfect pitch has a number of advantages. For example, this particular person has memorized her Zip Code and telephone number by humming them. When I heard her do this, it was the first time I had ever heard a Zip Code or a telephone number hummed. She assigns middle C the value of 1, C sharp 2, D 3, and so forth in order to know which number gets which pitch. Obviously she has a very strong auditory channel.

5. If money is not a problem, does your friend prefer to call a relative long distance or to send a card on a birthday? Usually the

strong auditory learner prefers to call and the strong visual learner prefers to write. This is not always true because sometimes money and even procrastination do enter in. An interesting thing to note here is that it would be more meaningful to the person who is having the birthday if we would make the decision to telephone or write a card depending on *that person's* strong learning channel. If that person is a strong auditory learner, he will usually appreciate a telephone call more than a birthday card. The reverse would be true for a strong visual learner.

The information provided in this appendix should be enough to enable you to discover your friend's strong learning channel. Remember that your decision should be a tentative one rather than a firm one. Go ahead and begin to work with the person as if the learning channel you have seen as strong is actually the strong one, but be willing to change your mind if you find evidence that you need to.

About the Author

PAUL WELTER, Ed.D., is a professor of counseling and educational psychology at Kearney State College, Nebraska. He is the author of *How to Help a Friend, Connecting with a Friend,* and *Learning from Children,* all published by Tyndale House.